The Great
Bridge-Building Contest

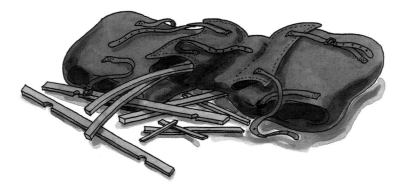

Bo Zaunders
Illustrated by Roxie Munro

HARRY N. ABRAMS, INC., PUBLISHERS

Artist's Note

The illustrations in this book are line drawings painted with a layered watercolor technique
using India and colored inks on 100 percent Strathmore cotton rag paper.

To my paternal grandparents, Esther Baird Chenoweth Munro and Robert MacGregor Munro
—R.M.

Production Manager: Jonathan Lopes

Library of Congress Cataloging-in-Publication Data
Zaunders, Bo.
The Great Bridge-Building Contest / Bo Zaunders ; illustrated by Roxie Munro.
p. cm.
ISBN 0-8109-4929-6
1. Chenoweth, Lemuel, 1811-1887—Juvenile literature. 2. Covered bridges—West Virginia—Philippi—History—19th century—Juvenile literature. 3. Civil engineers—West Virginia—Biography—Juvenile literature. 4. Architects—West Virginia—Biography—Juvenile literature. 5. Bridges—West Virginia—Design and construction—History—19th century—Juvenile literature. 6. Philippi (W. Va.)—History—19th century—Juvenile literature. 7. West Virginia—History—Civil War, 1861–1865—Juvenile literature. 8. Beverly (W. Va.)—Biography—Juvenile literature. I. Munro, Roxie. II. Title.

TG25.P58Z38 2004
624.2'18'0975459—dc22

2004001757

Published in 2004 by Harry N. Abrams, Incorporated, New York.

Printed and bound in China
10 9 8 7 6 5 4 3 2 1

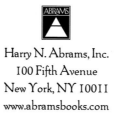

Harry N. Abrams, Inc.
100 Fifth Avenue
New York, NY 10011
www.abramsbooks.com

Abrams is a subsidiary of

LA MARTINIÈRE
GROUPE

Long ago in America, before the automobile, travel was slow, difficult, and unpredictable. In the early 1800s there were few highways. People traveled on narrow roads of dirt or stone, or on simple trails the width of one horse. When they came to a stream or small river, they were unlikely to find a bridge. There might be a spot to wade across or a small ferry, if they were lucky. A twenty-mile buggy ride on what was considered a good road was likely to turn into a full day's journey. But, by mid-century, things started to change. The invention of the steam engine led to the beginning of the railroads. Then came the construction of roads, highways, and bridges. With each passing decade, Americans could travel more freely throughout their vast young nation. It was a century of phenomenal progress, as well as wrenching political upheaval. An era of great engineers, it produced a number of outstanding bridge builders. These were often men of little education, but with lots of good old American know-how.

This is the story of one such man.

The new north-south highway in western Virginia had come to a stop in the small town of Philippi on the Tygart River, where there was only a small ferry crossing. The bustling thoroughfare needed a bridge.

But who would build it? In time-honored fashion, the Board of Public Works in Richmond, the state capital, announced a competition, open to anyone. Notices were posted and put in the newspapers. A date was set for when the board would review the various proposals.

TO
Bridge Builders.

For Sale

For Sale

On an early July morning in 1850, contestants began to arrive in Richmond. They were all construction experts. Some were experienced stone-masons (builders specializing in the laying of stone and brick), others skillful carpenters, and several were engineers, experts in technology, with university degrees. They came from all over the eastern United States—some from as far away as Boston, Massachusetts. A few traveled by train, which was still somewhat of a novelty. Others arrived in hired carriages or in their own horse-drawn buggies.

But for cabinetmaker Lemuel Chenoweth from the small village of Beverly, in the rocky hills of northwestern Virginia, there was no such luxury.

To Lemuel, the bridge contest was a dreamed-of opportunity. He already had some experience building bridges, but nothing comparable to this. With seven children and a pregnant wife, he could ill afford to take time off from making furniture. Still, he had spent months pondering what kind of bridge he would build. Nothing must be left to chance, every detail must be carefully worked out. After toiling all day in his workshop, he continued the problem-solving process at the kitchen table, deep into the night, when everyone else was sound asleep. It was a labor of love. To Lemuel a bridge must be both functional and beautiful.

Now, strapping two leather saddlebags to his only horse, he set out on what would be a long, hard journey. In the mid-nineteenth century, West Virginia was still part of Virginia; and to reach Richmond, Lemuel first had to cross the Allegheny Mountains. After that, he rode through the Shenandoah Valley until he reached the Blue Ridge Mountains. Even then, he was only halfway there. Next came the broad, rolling landscape of the Piedmont. It was a 200-mile trip, and it took him well over a week. Sometimes, as evening fell, he found a boarding house or a farmer willing to put him up for the night. But most often he would just wrap himself up in a blanket and sleep by the roadside.

When he finally arrived in Richmond, dusty and disheveled, it was late afternoon, and there was barely time for him to get to the meeting.

The State House conference room was in a flurry of activity. One bridge model after another was unwrapped and put on display. These were magnifcent models indeed, supreme examples of the technological advances of the day, representing a wide variety of bridge types. Many had been meticulously painted and decorated. Some even had panels with enameled inlays.

The bridge would have to support wagonloads of heavy goods, such as grain or timber, and large herds of livestock, so special attention was paid to strength. Along with the models came rolled-up, painstakingly drawn blueprints in which each bidder set forth his claim of what weight his bridge could sustain.

One by one, the contestants showed their ideas and explained their plans to the four-member Board of Public Works:

"As you can see, gentlemen, this is a rather light structure, in which iron cables, suspended from two towers and anchored at either end, leap from one side to the other and hold up the bridge—a wire cable suspension bridge, in other words . . ."

"In this cantilever bridge, the span is formed by two arms, fixed to the shores, and meeting in the middle."

"To keep the wooden beams and arches from being exposed to the elements, it is essential that this bridge be covered with a roof..."

"The massive arch, you'll note, diverts the load of the bridge to the ground on each side..."

Finally, as the presentations came to a close, there was only Lemuel left.

As Lemuel unloaded his saddlebags and took out a bunch of oak sticks wrapped in old newspapers, chuckles of amusement rippled through the assembly. What on earth was this lanky country bumpkin up to? Was this some kind of a joke?

Quietly, Lemuel assembled a miniature bridge. He used no hammer, no nails. Compared to the others, his model was plain indeed, unpainted and with no fine detailing. At last, in front of a scornful audience, he pulled out two ladder-backed chairs from a conference table, placed his construction across them, turned to the board, and spoke for the first time.

"Since I have no blueprints," he said, "you may allow me a demonstration."

Suddenly, using the rung of the chair, he stepped onto the top of the model, and walked across it—from one end to the other. A gasp went through the audience. No way could it hold! Each one of them knew their mathematics. Had this been the actual bridge it would have been as if a six-hundred-foot man stood on it.

But the model held.

In the hushed silence that followed Lemuel turned to the other engineers and quietly asked, "Can you stand on your models?"

Of course, no one dared. They all knew their models would be crushed.

And that's how Lemuel Chenoweth, a shy western Virginian with a third-grade education, won the competition.

As work on the bridge began, Lemuel chose a friend, a well-known stonemason, to supervise the building of its stone piers, twin foundations sunk deep into the river bottom. The plan called for a giant wooden structure, longer than a football field with not one but two roadways and a roof for protection. A wooden bridge, unlike one of iron or stone, might deteriorate from rain or snow.

With mathematical precision and without any drawings to go by, Lemuel worked out every little detail in his head. Huge yellow poplar trees were cut near the site. The logs were hand hewn and then carefully fitted together with wooden pins—the only ironworks being a few necessary bolts made by the local ironsmith.

The proceedings were followed closely by all the
townspeople. After all, this was their bridge.
When it was finished two years later, in 1852, it
quickly became the pride of Philippi, and the
wonder of the whole region.

The bridge was a boon to travelers. Local fishermen used it as shelter from the rain. And to the small boys of the community, the bridge was a source of constant joy. In the choking dust inside, perched in safety atop its rafters, they would watch as crowds of bawling cattle were herded by dogs from one side to the other. There was always a chance that a steer, frightened by the darkness, might suddenly turn, and, with lowered horns, charge one of the dogs and create confusion, even a stampede. A tollgate was placed at one end of the bridge, with a posting of the fees.

FOR EVERY HORSE AND RIDER...10 CENTS

FOR EVERY LED OR DRIVEN HORSE.....................................15 CENTS

FOR ALL 2 OR FOR 4 WHEELED WAGONS DRAWN BY 1 HORSE...........20 CENTS

FOR EVERY STAGE DRAWN BY 4 HORSES.................................50 CENTS

FOR EVERY HEAD OF CATTLE..01 1/2 C

FOR SCORE OF SHEEP..05 CENTS

FOR SCORE OF HOGS...10 CENTS

Business flourished. Then everything changed when war broke out in the spring of 1861.

For years, there had been increased tension between America's northern and southern states. As the South remained agricultural, depending on slave labor for its economy, the North had become more and more industrialized, with factories creating thousands of new jobs. The split was a threat to the Union, which Abraham Lincoln, the newly elected president, was anxious to preserve. Despite his efforts, the South decided to break away, and formed its own Confederate Army. This marked the beginning of the Civil War, the strife that nearly tore the country apart.

Because of its location, right between the North and South, Philippi Bridge immediately became a prize to both the Confederate and the Union armies. It was first occupied by a small group of Confederate soldiers who, lacking ammunition, panicked and ran when attacked by Union forces. The chase that followed was the first land battle of the Civil War, and is often referred to as the Philippi Races. Union troops subsequently seized the bridge, used it for barracks, and then received orders to burn it down along with other bridges in western Virginia. For all its "giant's strength and size," Lemuel is quoted as having said, it was "helpless against so small a thing as a match." Fortunately, townspeople intervened, and the bridge was saved.

According to local legend, President Lincoln, in an effort to put an end to the war, once held a secret meeting at the bridge with Jefferson Davis, the head of the Confederacy. If such a meeting took place, it certainly wasn't successful. The fighting dragged on for nearly five years, at the staggering cost of some 620,000 American lives.

A century and a half later, Lemuel's bridge,
having survived a war, floods, and an accidental
fire in 1989, is still used, and now holds the
distinction of being the nation's only covered
bridge serving a federal highway. Long gone are
the horse-drawn wagons, the bawling cattle, and
the squealing hogs. Boys no longer perch atop its
dusty rafters, and fishermen are less likely to use it
for keeping dry. Instead of bleating sheep, it has
trucks roaring through its dark interior. The
traffic load is many times heavier than
its builder possibly could have
imagined back in 1850. But
anything Lemuel built, he
built to last.

Lemuel Chenoweth is still a celebrated name in West Virginia. Historical plaques line the highways; the Philippi Museum, next to the famous bridge, abounds with Chenoweth memorabilia; and the homestead he built in Beverly in 1856 has been turned into a museum. In 1983, West Virginia Governor Jay Rockefeller declared June 15 Lemuel Chenoweth Day.

A Brief Biography of Lemuel Chenoweth

Lemuel Chenoweth was born in 1811 and lived his entire life in Beverly, West Virginia. His three years of formal education took place in a one-room log cabin. He learned calculus from a prominent surveyor, but was essentially a self-taught engineer and architect. He started out designing furniture, wagons, coffins, and cabinetry. Later, he built houses, a church, and many bridges—several of which he rebuilt after they were destroyed in the Civil War. Lemuel made his own tools and, though he often collaborated with stonemasons and ironsmiths, he supervised all the woodwork himself.

At age twenty-five he had married fourteen-year-old Nancy Hart, the great-granddaughter of John Hart, one of the signers of the Declaration of Independence. They had thirteen children.

Like many western Virginians, he was pro-South, but, generally, tried to stay out of the war. Two of his sons fought in the Confederate Army, and one of them, Joseph, was killed at Port Republic in 1862, while serving as an officer under Stonewall Jackson. During the war, Union soldiers were billeted in the Chenoweth house in Beverly. One married Lemuel's daughter Harriet Elisabeth. After the war, Lemuel became actively involved with the political and civic affairs of what, in 1863, had become the new state of West Virginia. He served as county coroner and as a member of the state legislature. He died in 1887, at age seventy-six.

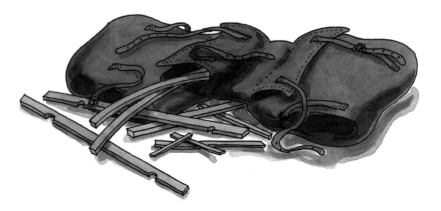

How did we hear about this story?

Zachary Taylor Chenoweth, Lemuel's seventh child, was artist Roxie Munro's great-grandfather, and all through her childhood she heard the story about her great-great-granddaddy Lemuel, the model bridge, and the two chairs.

The Covered Bridge

The wooden covered bridge is an American icon. It was the most popular type of bridge in the 1800s. Between 1805 and 1885 more than 10,000 covered bridges were built in the United States. Over ninety percent of them are now gone, and those that remain are treasured for their rustic charm and historical value.

The following is a small selection of covered bridges still in existence.

ARTIST'S COVERED BRIDGE
NEWRY, MAINE

No covered bridge in Maine—there are nine—is more photographed and painted than this one. Thus the name: the Artist's Covered Bridge. It is located about four miles northwest of North Bethel.

SWIFT RIVER BRIDGE
CONWAY, NEW HAMPSHIRE

Spanning the Swift River, this bridge was constructed in 1870. Applying Yankee thrift, the builders used timber salvaged from two other bridges, both destroyed a year earlier in a spring flood.

GREEN RIVER BRIDGE
GUILFORD, VERMONT

This bridge, constructed in 1873 and spanning the Green River, is unusual in that it has mailboxes inside.

CODDING BRIDGE
WATERVILLE, VERMONT

This classic Vermont bridge from 1877 is known as the "Kissing Bridge," because a visitor put up a sign that said so. Because of the privacy they afforded, covered bridges were often called "Kissing Bridges."

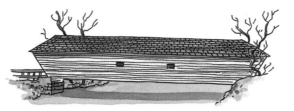

ELIZABETHTON COVERED BRIDGE
CARTER COUNTY, TENNESSEE

Located in downtown Elizabethton, this bridge, constructed in 1882, is adjacent to a park and spans the Doe River. It has become a focal point and a well-known landmark in the state of Tennessee.

PARADISE BRIDGE
LANCASTER COUNTY, PENNSYLVANIA

This 1893 bridge, crossing the Pequea Creek, leads to Paradise, a small village east of Lancaster city. If you visit it, expect the clip-clop of horse's hooves on its wooden floor. This is in the heart of Amish country, where buggies are still fashionable.

BLENHEIM COVERED BRIDGE
SCHOHARIE COUNTY, NEW YORK

When it was near completion in 1855, local experts predicted that this bridge would fall of its own weight, calling it "Powers's Folly," after the builder, Nicholas Montgomery Powers. To show that he was not in the least worried, Powers clambered to the top of his masterpiece as the workmen began knocking away the supporting timber. The bridge creaked but settled comfortably. The crowd cheered, and Powers just sat there, grinning.

ROSEMAN COVERED BRIDGE
MADISON COUNTY, IOWA

In 1892, a county jail escapee, pursued by two sheriffs, was trapped on this bridge. Uttering a wild cry, he went through the roof, literally, and disappeared forever. The general verdict was that anyone capable of such a feat must be innocent, and the bridge became known as the "haunted bridge." Built in 1883, it was the setting for *The Bridges of Madison County*, a famous novel that became a movie of the same name.

ZUMBROTA BRIDGE
ZUMBROTA, MINNESOTA

The Zumbrota Bridge is Minnesota's only authentic covered bridge left today. It was built in 1857, and has a sign on it that says, "$10 fine for traveling faster than a walk over this bridge." A park next to it features Kid's Kingdom, a gigantic children's playground.

OTWAY BRIDGE
SCIOTO COUNTY, OHIO

Spanning the Scioto Brush Creek, the Otway Bridge gained celebrity status before it was even completed, in 1873. One of the workers, a daring young man, decided to show off by walking on stilts along the top chords of the bridge—making it safely to the other side.

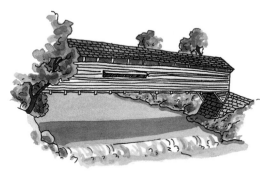

UNION COVERED BRIDGE
PARIS, MISSOURI

About thirty covered bridges once spanned Missouri's rivers and creeks. Now there are four, one of which is the Union Covered Bridge. Built in 1871, it sits in a very picturesque location, spanning the Elk Fork of the Salt River. It is now closed to traffic but open to pedestrians.

REXLEIGH COVERED BRIDGE
WASHINGTON COUNTY, NEW YORK

Like the Zumbrota Bridge, this one has a warning sign: "$25 fine for driving on this bridge faster than a walk." Listed on the National Register of Historic Places, the Rexleigh Bridge is located in the town of Jackson Salem, and crosses the Battenkill River. It was built in 1874.

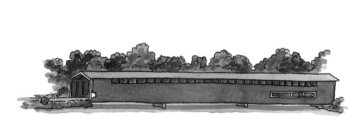

LANGLEY COVERED BRIDGE
ST. JOSEPH COUNTY, MICHIGAN

This is the longest of West Michigan's few remaining covered bridges, stretching 232 feet across the St. Joseph River. Built in 1887, it is located three miles north of Centreville on County Route 133, and named for Thomas W. Langley, Centreville's first settler.

SWITZER BRIDGE
FRANKLIN COUNTY, KENTUCKY

There are twelve remaining covered bridges in Kentucky, including the Switzer Bridge. Built originally in 1855, it was restored in 1906 and, after it was knocked from its foundation in the spring of 1997, rebuilt yet again. A Switzer Covered Bridge Day is celebrated annually, on the last Saturday in September.

BLAIR BRIDGE
CAMPTON, NEW HAMPSHIRE

A doctor trying to ford the strong currents of the Pemigewasset River on horseback brought about the construction of the Blair Bridge in 1869. The horse drowned, but the doctor was saved. Immediately, the citizens of Campton decided to build a bridge.

HUMPBACK BRIDGE
ALLEGHANY COUNTY, VIRGINIA

This 100-foot long structure got its name because it is four feet higher at its center than it is at either end. Contemporary with Lemuel's bridge in Philippi, the Humpback Bridge was built in 1857, and stretches across the Dunlap Creek, a tributary of the Jackson River.

WEST CORNWALL BRIDGE
LITCHFIELD COUNTY, CONNECTICUT

This is one of two remaining covered bridges in Connecticut. Crossing the Housatonic River, it was constructed in 1864 on the site of an earlier bridge. In 1973, a concealed steel roof was installed and the bridge was raised two feet for protection against floodwaters.

KNOX BRIDGE
VALLEY FORGE NATIONAL HISTORICAL PARK, PENNSYLVANIA

In the 1800s, a record number of about 1,500 covered bridges were built in Pennsylvania. Of the 217 that still remain, the Knox Bridge is one of the most distinctive and most often visited. It spans the Valley Creek, just off State Route 252.